Prince With a Paintbrush

THE STORY OF RAJA RAVI VARMA

For my mother, Lily, who wished that
I would be a painter, a potter, a poet ... all three!

First published by Red Panda, an imprint of Westland Publications Private Limited, in 2021

Published by Red Panda, an imprint of Westland Books, a division of Nasadiya Technologies Private Limited, in 2023

No. 269/2B, First Floor, 'Irai Arul', Vimalraj Street, Nethaji Nagar, Alapakkam Main Road, Maduravoyal, Chennai 600095

Westland, the Westland logo, Red Panda and the Red Panda logo are the trademarks of Nasadiya Technologies Private Limited, or its affiliates.

We would like to thank Raja Ravi Varma Heritage Foundation for images and information.
Image credits in order of their appearance in the book *Descent of Ganga* (oleograph) - Collection of Sandeep & Gitanjali Maini Foundation; *Goddess Saraswati* - Collection of Maharaja Fateh Singh Museum, Baroda; Ravi Varma's Studio in Kilimanoor - Collection of Jay Varma; *Kerala Royal Lady* (attributed to Raja Ravi Varma) - Private collection; *Madri (Maharashtrian Lady With Fruit)* - Travancore Royal Family, Kaudiar; *Malabar Lady* - Private collection; *Nair Lady Arranging Jasmine in Her Hair* - Travancore Royal Family, Kaudiar; *Goddess Saraswati* - Collection of Maharaja Fateh Singh Museum, Baroda; *Goddess Lakshmi* (Lithographic Print) - Private collection; *Introducing Radha to Krishna* (Lithographic Print) - Collection of Sandeep & Gitanjali Maini Foundation; *Jatayu Vadh* - Shri Jayachamarjendra Art Gallery Trust, Mysore; *Bishop Geeverghese Mar Gregorious of Parumala* - Collection of Saint John's Attamangalam, Jacobite Syrian Church, Kumarakom; *There Comes Papa* - Travancore Royal Family, Kaudiar; *Portrait of Maharaja Sayaji Rao of Baroda* - Collection of Maharaja Fateh Singh Museum, Baroda; *Galaxy of Musicians* - Shri Jayachamarajendra Art Gallery Trust, Mysore; *Portrait of Raja Ravi Varma* by Mangalabai Tampuratty - Madhavan Nair Foundation, Kochi

ISBN:9789357768153

Book design by New Media Line Creations, New Delhi 110 062

Printed at Saurabh Printers Pvt. Ltd.

Prince With a Paintbrush

THE STORY OF RAJA RAVI VARMA

Shobha Tharoor Srinivasan

Illustrated by
Rayika Sen

RED PANDA

In school today, Mrs Mitra asked the class if anyone could name a famous artist. I was excited. I raised my hand and said, 'Vincent van Gogh.' I remembered that beautiful framed painting in Appa's office—*The Starry Night*—with its inky blue and black swirls. Mrs Mitra smiled at me.

Then she asked if anyone had heard of a famous Indian artist. Aarti raised her hand and said, 'I know. Raja Ravi Varma.' Mrs Mitra looked very pleased.

I hadn't heard of this artist before. He was a 'Raja'? That's unusual. Raja means king. Was he royalty? So interesting. I couldn't wait to get home and ask Amma to help me find some information about this artist.

Amma was excited about the project as well. She remembered some prints of this artist's work in her Ammamma's house in Palakkad, in Kerala. When she was young, she thought those pictures were all movie posters. Later, she learnt that those colourful pictures were characters from mythological stories. They were all reprints of paintings by Ravi Varma.

Amma and I sat down at our computer and decided to look up this painter on the internet. I learned that Ravi Varma was born in 1848, in the village of Kilimanoor, in Kerala.

Kilimanoor Palace

When Ravi Varma was a child, he loved to draw. Just like I do.

His parents often found him drawing and colouring on the walls.

It was good that Ravi's poet mother, Umayamba Thampuratty, and his Sanskrit scholar father, Neelakanthan Bhattatiripad, were happy about their son's creativity on the walls of the house. We read that he drew animals and ordinary people like the household and kitchen staff and the gardeners.

Ravi Varma was a lucky boy. His uncle Rajaraja Varma, who was a painter, noticed his nephew's obvious talent for art. He showed Ravi how to draw figures on the ground using something called quicklime. Amma said it is like the chalk I use for drawing on the floor with my friends.

Later his uncle prepared paints made from leaves, flowers, tree bark and soil for him. What a fun way to make colour! Ravi Varma's first set of oil paints were bought much later, from the big city of Madras. He was both nervous and excited to use them.

When Ravi was 14, his uncle Rajaraja Varma took him to the palace of the Maharaja of Travancore to observe and study under the palace painter, Ramaswami Naidu. Ravi started with learning watercolour painting. Later, when the Maharaja hired the Danish-born British artist, Theodor Jenson, to paint his portrait, Ravi Varma was able to observe and study the craft of oil painting.

Ravi Varma painted people just as he saw them. This style was influenced by the techniques of European 'Realism' that he had learned from his teacher. This means that he painted people exactly like they looked, without adding or highlighting anything. This painting of the lady in a white and gold sari was how women dressed in Kerala. So Ravi Varma may have painted the portrait using his mother or a grown-up friend as a model. He painted many paintings of Kerala women since he knew them best.

Kerala Royal Lady

Ravi Varma was the most successful Indian painter to start using this realistic style of painting. He was also one of the first to use oil paints on canvas.

The Indian artists before him painted in what was called the 'company style', since many of them worked for patrons in the British East India Company or other foreign companies. This art style was a blend of Mughal and English styles, in which the men and women on the canvas had a flat, one-dimensional look. You wouldn't feel like the person could step right out of the portrait, as in Ravi Varma's painting, *Kerala Royal Lady*. In this painting, we can see the folds of the woman's sari and the thoughtful expression in her eyes. Influenced by the Italian Renaissance painters, Ravi Varma drew and painted the human body just like it was. He painted fabrics, textures and materials clearly, with striking contrasts.

Amma said that Raja Ravi Varma's work marked a turning point in Indian art. We read that his work is a 'fusion of Indian aesthetics with techniques from the West.' Amma explained that his paintings had a little bit of both the Indian and European art styles. His style was similar to the European painters, but the subjects of his paintings were the Indian people he knew.

Madri (Maharashtrian Lady with Fruit)

He painted the people in everyday clothes and jewellery, making his art different and special.

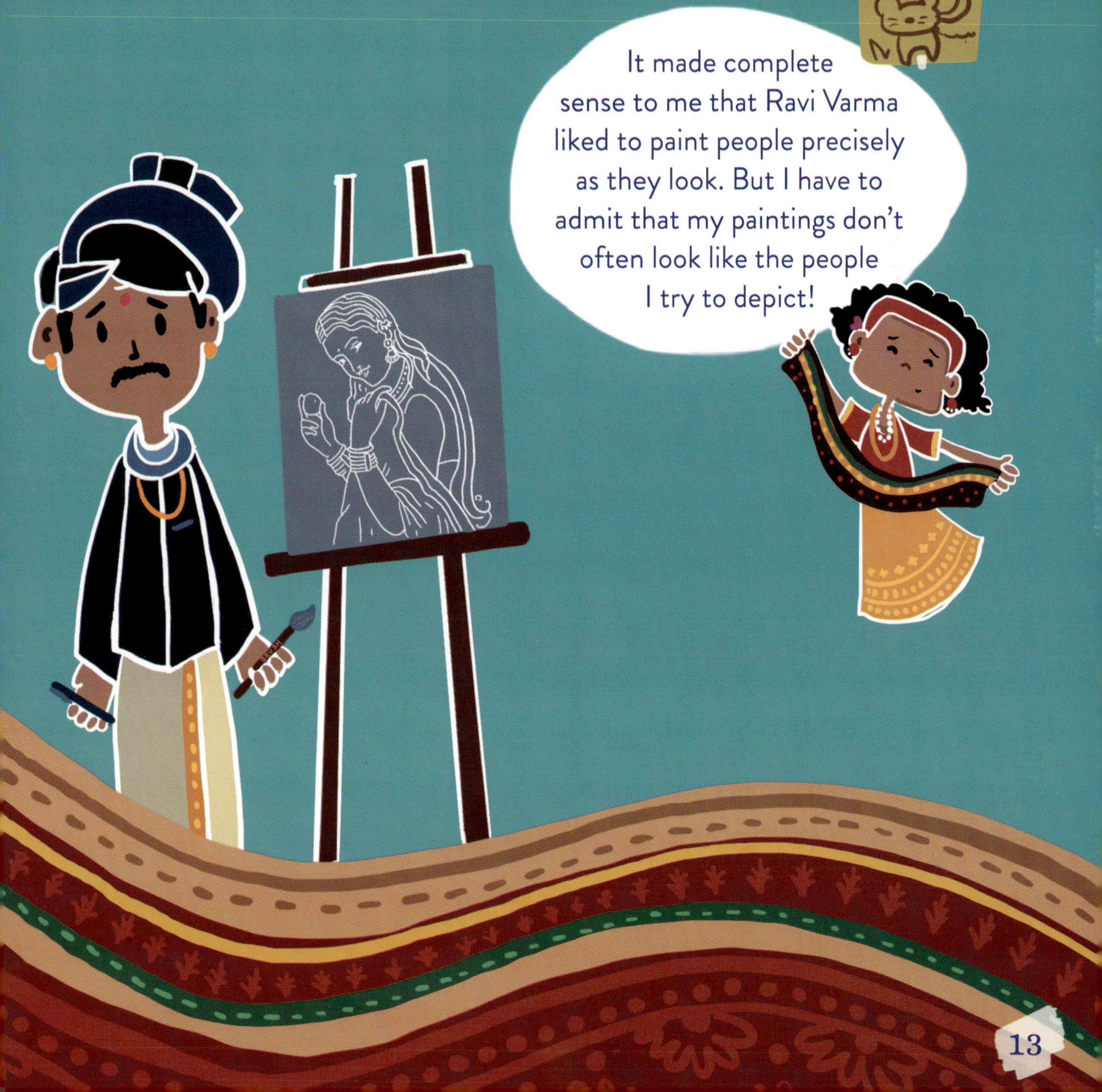

In the olden days, people got married early. When he was just eighteen years old, Ravi Varma's parents married him off to Rani Bhageerathi Bayi, a twelve-year-old princess of the Mavelikkara Royal House.

Being married meant that Ravi Varma needed to be responsible and have a full-time job. He decided to be a painter and worked hard. Using oil paints, he learned to master his techniques on canvas.

He began his career painting portraits of the important local people that he knew. Since his paintings were so amazing, he was soon hired to do oil paintings for the Royal Court of Travancore.

Malabar Lady Playing The Veena

Amma said that Ravi Varma worked hard and followed a strict daily routine. He would wake up at four o'clock every morning to say his prayers. At six o'clock, when the sun was just coming up, he would start working on his art. He painted every day till five in the evening. Only then would he play with his children or be with his wife or friends.

Amma believed that all the hard work led to Ravi Varma's success. I knew Amma would say that! I bet he wouldn't have been so successful if he didn't have people cooking his meals for him and keeping his house clean!

Nair Lady Adorning Her Hair

The painting, *Nair Lady Adorning Her Hair*, was awarded the first prize, the Governor's gold medal, at the Madras Fine Arts Society exhibition, in 1873. It made Ravi Varma a famous man. The painting was shown in Europe, where it received a Certificate of Merit at an international exhibition held in Vienna. It was a big achievement since so many other painters took part, and the competition was tough. Ravi Varma was only twenty-five years old when he won the award.

His paintings were also sent to the World's Columbian Exposition, held in Chicago, in 1893. He was awarded three gold medals there as well.

Soon, travel became a regular activity for Ravi Varma. He travelled all over India and considered it a part of his cultural growth. The women he met during his travel became the subjects of his early paintings. I read that some of his paintings had multiple versions of the same women.

Towards the end of the 1800s, Ravi Varma decided to change his focus and use real men and women as models for gods and goddesses in his art. Every image he painted continued to have a three-dimensional look. And the gods and goddesses he painted looked like real people who lived in the real world.

This painting of Goddess Saraswati is so beautiful. Look at her face. She looks like she could walk right out of the painting, doesn't she?

Goddess Saraswati

And look at the bright colours that Ravi Varma used to create this painting of Goddess Lakshmi. The face looks so real.

I read that Ravi Varma often modelled Hindu goddesses on South Indian women, whom he considered beautiful. This painting could even be my mother, all dressed up.

We found four different versions of Goddess Lakshmi paintings when we looked online.

Goddess Lakshmi

Ravi Varma also painted male gods in a realistic style, with bodies like that of real people.

In this painting, Radha is meeting Lord Krishna for the first time.

Introducing Radha to Krishna

I told Amma that Ravi Varma's paintings reminded me of the pictures in *Amar Chitra Katha*. Is it possible that the creators of *Amar Chitra Katha* comic books were inspired by Ravi Varma's style and used it in their artwork? Amma said that Raja Ravi Varma was, in fact, the first person to paint the characters from many stories that I had read in those comics. Ravi Varma used the portraits of the people he knew to depict the characters in the stories from Hindu mythology. He painted stories about Dushyanta and Shakuntala, Nala and Damayanti, Krishna and Radha, and Rama and Sita and their adventures. I've read comics of all these stories.

During the last years of the 19th century and in the early years of the 20th century, Ravi Varma was the most famous artist in India. He was well regarded both as a portrait-maker and as a creator and storyteller of Indian mythology.

Look at this amazing painting of a scene from the Ramayana that shows Ravana's cruel expression as he clips one of the wings of the brave bird, Jatayu.

Jatayu Vadh

My mother said that Ravi Varma painted gods with a human touch. They seemed friendly enough, just like people.

He didn't only paint Hindu gods; he painted people of all faiths. This portrait of the Bishop of Kerala, also painted by Ravi Varma, hangs in a church in Kerala.

Bishop Geevarghese Mar Gregorios of Parumala

Ravi Varma and his wife had three daughters and two sons. This is a painting that Ravi Varma made of his daughter, Mahaprabha, holding her son, RM Varma, in her arms.

There Comes Papa

I read that Ravi Varma lived in a time when people in India were looking for creative ways to free themselves from British rule. Ravi Varma's bright and dazzling paintings of India's past made people feel proud of their history and literature. This made his paintings very popular, and people wanted to have their portraits painted by him.

In his later years, Ravi Varma lived in states outside of Kerala. He lived in Mysore in Karnataka, in Baroda in Gujarat, and several other cities in India.

In 1881, the Maharaja of Baroda, Sayajirao Gaekwad, invited Ravi Varma to his Lakshmi Vilas Palace in Baroda to be a resident artist. During his stay there, he painted many canvases that told stories from the Mahabharata and Ramayana. He also created many portraits of the members of the Baroda royal family. Ravi Varma stayed in Gujarat for nearly fourteen years.

Portrait of Maharaja Sayaji Rao of Baroda

In 1888, Ravi Varma went on an all-India tour to get an idea of the different clothes worn by men and women in other parts of the country. This change of setting helped him think and paint differently. He shared many folk and traditional art forms of India on canvas, and his art no longer just used South Indian models.

Galaxy of Musicians

Ravi Varma became such a famous Indian artist because he made sure his art could be appreciated by everyone, not just by rich people who could buy expensive canvases. In 1894, he started a lithography press called the Ravi Varma Pictures Depot in Maharashtra and made many, many copies of his paintings so that more people could see and own the beautiful art, and worship God inside their own houses. Ravi Varma asked his brother Rajaraja Varma to manage the press. But since it lost him money, he sold it to a German printing technician. In 1901, a mysterious fire destroyed the press and it had to be shut down temporarily.

In 1904, the Viceroy of India, Lord Curzon, gave Ravi Varma, the Kaisar-i-Hind Gold Medal as a recognition by the British Empire, to acknowledge his artistic talent. He was also given the title 'Raja'. And, from then on, Ravi Varma was called Raja Ravi Varma.

Two years later, Raja Ravi Varma passed away, at the age of 58. He was fondly remembered as the 'Leonardo Da Vinci of India'. It was said that by combining Indian traditions and Indian subjects with European techniques, Raja Ravi Varma had created a new style of painting in India. He would never be forgotten.

Raja Ravi Varma's style influenced many artists after him. Amma said that today he is regarded as the most important representative of the Europeanised school of art in India.

I took out my scrapbook and cut out and stuck this portrait of Raja Ravi Varma in it.

MY SCRAPBOOK

ENTRY: RAJA RAVI VARMA

DETAILS: BORN: 29 APRIL 1848

DIED: 2 OCTOBER 1906

OCCUPATION: PAINTER, ARTIST

FROM: TRAVANCORE

POTRAIT OF RAJA RAVI VARMA

I then wrote a short poem about him:

Raja Ravi Varma,
the Prince from Travancore,
Was known for his great
paintings, of Indian epic-lore.
His strokes were bright and
vibrant.
He created them with style.
People rushed to buy his
work,
And he made it worth their
while.

I can't wait to tell Mrs Mitra that I know so much about the artist Raja Ravi Varma!

More Cool Facts About Raja Ravi Varma

Raja Ravi Varma's art was appreciated by the British. They often invited him and his brother Rajaraja Varma to parties at their homes. The family also socialised with British friends at their home in Kilimanoor.

Raja Ravi Varma was SO famous that his birthplace, the small town of Kilimanoor, had to open a post office because letters and requests for paintings came flooding in from various corners of the country!

Raja Ravi Varma was SO important that the government of Kerala created an award in his name known as the 'Raja Ravi Varma Puraskaram'.

Raja Ravi Varma was SO great that in 2013, a crater on planet Mercury was named 'Varma', in his honour!

In 2008, a sari, woven with copies of eleven paintings by Raja Ravi Varma entered the *Guinness Book of World Records* as the most expensive silk sari, globally. The sari was priced at Rs 40 lakh and weighed 8 kgs! The main highlight of the sari is Ravi Varma's famous painting *Galaxy of Musicians*. It had taken 36 weavers a whole year to hand-weave this 'vivaah-patu' or wedding sari!

Raja Ravi Varma's sister Mangala Bayi and brother Rajaraja Varma also had artistic talent. They both assisted their brother at times. Rajaraja Varma often painted the backdrops and landscapes in RRV's paintings, and Mangala Bayi helped with the facial expressions. Unfortunately, it was not easy for a woman to be a professional artist in those times, so Mangala Bayi could not become as famous as her brother. RRV also had another brother called Goda Varma, who led a private life.

Raja Ravi Varma's youngest son Rama Varma was his only child who studied art. He studied at the JJ School of Arts in Mumbai and became an artist.

Dadasaheb Phalke, known as the father of Indian cinema, worked at the Ravi Varma Press in the early 20th century. When Phalke moved to the movie industry, he used what he had seen in the press to create artwork for movie posters. This is why so many Bollywood posters with their bright colours look just like Raja Ravi Varma paintings.

Ravi Varma's first trip away from home was to the Mukambika temple in western Kerala, in 1870, when he was 22 years old. He often travelled with a cook so that he could eat the food that he liked eating!

Bala Saheb, the Prince of Audh, admired Ravi Varma very much. His devotion for the artist was so deep that he saw Ravi Varma almost as a God and kept the artist's photograph in his prayer room!

Meet the Author

Shobha Tharoor Srinivasan is an award-winning voice-over artist, poet, editor and author of a dozen works of fiction and non-fiction. She is also a former nonprofit development professional who spent two decades as an advocate and fundraiser for persons with disabilities. She won the 68th National Film Awards for Best Narration Voiceover for the film *Rhapsody of Rains - Monsoons of Kerala*, in 2022.

Shobha has published children's books in India and the United States, including the award-winning *Indi-Alphabet, A Treasure Trove of Timeless Tales* (Westland), *It's Time to Rhyme* and *Parvati the Elephant's Very Important Day.*

Her first book for adults, *Good Innings*, and *A Treasure Trove of Timeless Tales* is being translated into Malayalam.

Shobha's love of words and stories began in childhood with storytelling sessions and word play with her siblings.

Meet the Illustrator

Rayika Sen, a graduate from Srishti School of Art, Design and Technology, is a toy designer, illustrator and storyteller who specialises in designing content for children. *Great Lives: Ruskin Bond, Scholastic Book of Hindu Gods and Goddesses, Samay Ka Khatola by Gulzar, The Dragon's Toothache* and *I Am Not Afraid* are some of the books that Rayika has illustrated. She has also created several craft books, including the Cool Crafts series.

Her works have been published in *Creative Gaga* magazine and *Deccan Herald* newspaper, and also featured in international forums like the Bologna Children's Book Fair and AFCC, Singapore.